The British Computer Society is the leading professional and learned society in the field of computers and information systems. Formed in 1957, it has approximately 38,000 members world-wide. The Society is concerned with the development of computing and its effective application. Under its Royal Charter, granted in 1984, it also has responsibilities for education and training, public awareness and above all standards, quality and professionalism.

The Society is also an Engineering Institution, with over 7,000 members registered as Incorporated and Chartered Engineers.

Through its structure of professional and non-professional grades the Society provides a unique service to all those concerned with information systems. BCS professional membership grades are a widely acknowledged demonstration of professional competence and its codes of practice set high standards of ethics and accountability.

Further information about the British Computer Society, including the requirements for membership and the services provided, can be obtained from:

Marketing Department
The British Computer Society
1 Sanford Street
Swindon
Wiltshire SN1 1HJ
Telephone 01793 417424
E-mail: bcs@hq.bcs.org.uk
Web: http://www.bcs.org.uk

This book was prepared by the Intellectual Property Rights Task Force of the Legal Affairs Committee of the British Computer Society which is chaired by Trevor Cook. Within the task force the editor who drew together the work was Michael Gifkins. The main focus of the book is upon law concerning Intellectual Property Rights (IPR) in the UK.

Members of the Task Force who contributed to the preparation of the book were:

Simon Chalton (Consultant solicitor with Bird & Bird, Solicitors)
Trevor Cook (Partner with Bird & Bird, Solicitors)
Michael Gifkins (Chartered Arbitrator and Consultant with Logica)
Derrick Grover (Independent Consultant)
Robert Hart (Patent Attorney)
Ian Lowe (Partner with Berwin Leighton, Solicitors)
Ron McQuaker (Director of Exxel Consultants Ltd.)
Brett Rowland (Lawyer with Lovells, Lawyers)
Adrian Sterling (Lecturer in IP law and Barrister)
Uma Suthersanen (Lecturer in IP law)

The BCS gratefully acknowledges the support of Bird & Bird, Solicitors, during the preparation of this report.

Intellectual Property Rights in Software
A Practical Guide for Professionals & Business Managers

Copyright © 2000 The British Computer Society & Contributors

All rights reserved. No part of this publication may be reproduced in any form except as permitted by the Copyright Designs and Patents Act 1988. Enquiries for permission to reproduce material should be directed to the publisher.

The British Computer Society, 1 Sanford Street, Swindon, Wiltshire SN1 1HJ

ISBN 1-902505-18-2

British Cataloguing in Publication Data
A CIP catalogue record for this book is available from the British Library

First Printed in February 2000
Printed & bound in the UK by Charlesworth

All trademarks are acknowledged to be the property of their respective owners.

Disclaimer
Although every care has been taken by all members of the BCS Legal Affairs Committee and the Intellectual Property Rights Task Force of The British Computer Society in the preparation of this publication, no warranty is given by the BCS Legal Affairs Committee nor Intellectual Property Rights Task Force and its members or The British Computer Society as Publisher as to the accuracy or completeness of the information contained within it and neither the BCS Legal Affairs Committee nor Intellectual Property Rights Task Force members nor The British Computer Society shall be responsible or liable for any loss or damage whatsoever arising by virtue of such information or any instructions or advice contained within this publication or by any of the aforementioned.

Preface

For very many members of the vast IT community almost the only professional property they own is Intellectual Property, mainly software in the widest sense of the term. Even for companies not directly in the software business, significant assets are often created in the form of software intended to serve the business and to give it competitive edge.

Good software is the product of time, effort and creativity, the result of the expenditure of labour and other resources, and of course the investment of money. If another, without permission, appropriates the fruit of that labour, it is in principle theft. Various laws, notably copyright, are intended to deter such misappropriation or provide recompense if it occurs.

It is easy to state the basic principle – applying it in practice is not. There are uncertainties in the application of the existing law, for example in the protection of what an EU Directive calls 'preparatory design material', and there is international pressure to change the law, for example by extending the grant of patents to computer programs as such.

Nonetheless, there are practical measures honest practitioners can take to protect their intellectual property and to guard against misplaced allegations of infringement. As the chartered professional institution directly concerned with Information Systems, the British Computer Society has a duty both to its members, most of whose livelihoods are affected, and, under its Royal Charter, to the wider public, to address such issues as these.

This booklet is not a substitute for professional advice, but it is hoped that it will promote a wider understanding of intellectual property matters as they affect the daily working lives of software developers, suppliers and users, and provide them with practical guidance on good day to day practice.

Ron McQuaker CEng FBCS
Past President of the BCS
Chairman, Legal Affairs Committee of the BCS

Contents

Legal protection for software – Intellectual Property Rights

Q1 **What is meant**	**by *software*?**

Software is a term used in both a narrow and broad sense. In the narrow sense (and as generally used in this guide), it covers computer programs and preparatory design materials for computer programs. In the broad sense it is (often loosely) used to cover any recorded form of digitised information. This includes, as well as computer programs, graphics, sound recordings, video recordings etc. Thus in its broadest sense software describes much information content which is distinct from any hardware (CD or video player for example) by which the recorded information is stored or brought to perception.

Q2 **What are**	***Intellectual Property Rights?***

Intellectual property rights (IPRs) are generally considered as relating to products of the mind. The term includes copyright, patents, trade marks, design rights and confidential information.

The fundamental idea behind IPRs is that those who have invested skill and effort in creating something which is of use to others should acquire rights in works which they have created. IPRs, in various forms, lie at the very basis of our industrial society. Traditionally they have been associated with engineered products and with written documents.

Nowadays some of the world's richest have achieved their wealth through marketing software. The traditional forms of IPRs have been adopted to protect software products. These forms have also changed a little, reflecting the distinctive nature of software.

Computer programs and databases must be *original* to be protected, and there are complex rules for determining this. Broadly, if there has been a real individual intellectual contribution there will be protection. Sound recordings and films do not have to be original to get protection, but they must not be mere copies of existing protected material.

In the context of international commercial law, IPRs are of great importance to organisations. It is in the main these organisations which own rights to software or which pay for licences to use software. Nevertheless, individuals themselves may be owners of rights. There are sections below which give some coverage to concerns in this area. In this BCS guide we have chosen to give prominence to the positions of individuals – either as users or creators of IPRs in software.

One important distinction between types of intellectual property rights lies in whether or not they have to be registered with some central (generally national) authority in order to take effect. Such registration may either be a simple administrative act or may involve examination by an authority to see whether the right merits registration. Information on registered rights can be determined by inspection and search of public registers (in principle, though it may be hard in practice). Examples of registered rights are patents, registered designs and registered trade marks.

In general registered rights can be infringed by third party activity which falls within their scope even if the third party has no knowledge of the right.

In contrast, unregistered rights exist without any registration or examination and so cannot be searched against. By and large they can only be infringed by activity which has some causal connection with the right or to the material that the unregistered rights protect. Examples of such rights are copyright, unregistered design right, confidential information and unregistered trade marks protected under the law of passing off, although in the last of these cases the right can be infringed without any causal link.

Protection of rights in software

The established ways to protect rights in software, which may be used in combination, are:

Contractual Terms

The typical form of contract that is used to protect software is the software licence, which specifies what can be done with software without infringing the IPRs, such as copyright. Such a contract may also seek to restrict a user's actions more than the IPRs alone would. Although there are limits to the extent to which such contracts are enforceable even against those with whom they are made. Moreover they are only enforceable against the other contracting party, and not, unlike IPRs, against third parties.

Copyright

Copyright is used to protect every type of software. When you open a shrink wrapped product you may give assent to taking a licence to use someone's copyright material. Copyright subsists automatically in any works, such as computer programs, that are original and are created by a 'qualifying person', a term which includes anyone resident in or a national of the UK. It is an infringement of copyright to do any 'restricted act' in relation to the copyright work without the licence of the copyright owner. One of the restricted acts of importance for software is that of reproduction, or the copying of the whole or a substantial part of the copyright work, which clearly covers making unauthorised copies of an item of software. Where only a small part of the program code is copied, or the 'structure and function' but not the code of a program is copied, it can be difficult to establish whether or not a 'substantial part' of the original program or design documentation has indeed been copied.

Within computer networks it is common for transient copies of software to be created; copies which exist for a brief time within computer memory or on a random access device. The UK law of copyright restricts the making of such copies.

Patent

Patents are available *for any inventions, whether products or processes, in all fields of technology, provided that they are new, involve an inventive step and are capable of industrial application.* However both the European Patent Convention, and the Patents Act 1977 in the UK, declare that *a ... program for a computer* is not an invention (along with for example methods of doing business, presentations of information, algorithms and mental acts). This is probably because they are not deemed to be *capable of industrial application*, or at least they were not so deemed over 20 years ago, when these measures were drafted. Both the convention and the Act then go on to qualify this, by providing that this exception only applies to the extent that a patent application relates to a computer program (or method of doing business etc.) *as such*. In practice, at least in the European Patent Office, the exception is now so narrowly construed that it is almost always possible to formulate a software related invention as patentable subject matter, so that any novel and non-obvious principles behind a program can be *claimed* in a granted patent and protected accordingly.

Trade secret / confidential information

Information which is confidential in nature and which is disclosed under conditions imposing an obligation of confidence is protected under the law of confidential information, even in the hands of third parties who may not have been a party to the original arrangement under which the information was impressed with the obligation of confidence. In some cases companies protect software concepts by keeping the software a trade secret between supplier and user.

A user can learn significant facts about a program from using it. If such a user is not under an obligation of confidence then such learned facts cannot be regarded as confidential and this sets practical limits to the protection afforded by the law.

Trade marks

Trade marks may be either unregistered (in which case the law used to protect them is known in the UK as that of passing off) or registered, which in the UK may be either nationally, under the Trade Marks Act 1994, or at the Community Trade Mark Office, in which case the resulting Community Trade Mark has effect throughout the European Union. The owner of a registered trade mark can stop any use of that mark in relation to the same kind of goods or services. The benefit of having a registered trade mark is that it is not necessary to demonstrate that one holds copyright in an item of software or that the alleged infringement is a copy – merely that one has a registration in the appropriate class that covers software (Class 9) and that the infringer is either using that mark or one confusingly similar to it for goods of the same class. Trade marks can also be used to protect software-related services.

Design rights

There are two main modes of design protection in the United Kingdom: registered design right and unregistered design right. Registered design law is traditionally reserved for new, eye-appealing, aesthetic industrial designs. The unregistered design right, on the other hand, offers protection to original, three-dimensional designs, irrespective of their visual or aesthetic quality. The unregistered design right also provides protection for the topography of semiconductor products, including the design of integrated circuits or chips.

It should be noted that design features which constitute a *method or principle of construction* are excluded under both the registered design and unregistered design laws. Furthermore, while the unregistered design right will extend protection to both aesthetic and functional designs, the registered design law excludes purely functional design features (i.e. features which are dictated solely by the function which the article has to perform.). In 1998, a new E.C. Directive on designs was adopted and the scope of design protection throughout the European Union, including the UK, will soon be amended. Under the Directive, a design means *the appearance of the whole or a part of a product resulting from the features of, in particular, the lines, contours, colours, shape, texture and/or materials of the product itself and/or its ornamentation.* Furthermore, design protection will be extended to industrial and handicraft items, complex products and their parts, packaging, get-up, graphic symbols and typographic typefaces. Computer programs are clearly excluded. Nevertheless, under the new definition, design protection may be available in the future for computer graphics and icons.

How, practically, is protection of IPRs obtained?

Q3	How do I	seek patent protection?

Patents are territorial rights which require to be individually sought by separate patent application in each country in which protection is required. There is **no such thing** as a world wide patent. A UK patent on its own has no effect on activities in the United States for example. There are some international treaties, such as the Patent Co-operation Treaty and the European Patent Convention for example, where a single application can result in a **bundle** of granted patents for the Contracting States designated in the application.

Patents are best handled by skilled professionals, such as UK Patent Attorneys or European Patent Attorneys, and in the UK the Chartered Institute of Patent Agents (**www.cipa.org.uk/index.htm**) will provide a list of qualified people in your area on application.

Q4	What rights	does a patent confer?

A patent confers an exclusive right to prevent others from making, selling (or otherwise disposing of) and/or importing a patented product or using a patented process or selling (or otherwise dealing with) or importing any products made by means of that process. It does not confer any rights on the owner to use the invention. A patent has a life of 20 years if all renewal fees are paid.

Q5	When should I	file a patent application?

To obtain patent protection an application must be lodged in the Patent Office **before** information on the invention is made available to the public. To be patentable an *invention* must be new, involve an inventive step and be capable of industrial application.

The term invention is not defined in the European Patent Convention or the UK Patents Act 1977 but some inventions are excluded from patent protection. Amongst these are *schemes, rules and methods for performing mental acts, playing games or doing business or programs for computers*. However, these inventions are only excluded to the extent that the patent relates to such subject matter as such. The European Patent Office Technical Board of Appeal has construed the exclusion of *Computer Programs* as such as excluding only those programs that do not provide a technical contribution.

Q6 | Who owns | the rights in a patent?

Only the inventor is entitled to a patent for his or her invention. If the invention is made jointly by two or more people, they may make a joint patent application. The general rule is subject to exception when an invention is made by an employee in the course of his or her duties, where the right to apply for and receive patent protection belongs to the employer. In the UK, employee compensation may be awarded if the patent is of outstanding benefit to the employer. An inventor may transfer or assign his or her rights in an invention to another person, who is then entitled to the grant of any patent on the invention. In certain circumstances patents may also be used as security for loans or venture capital.

Q7 | How do I | obtain a patent?

The procedure for obtaining a patent involves the making of a patent application identifying to the Patent Office the applicant (who will become the owner of the patent when granted) and the inventors (in the sense of the actual devisors) of the invention. The patent application must also include a written enabling disclosure of the invention which is referred to as the patent specification. Upon the reception of a patent application the Patent Office issues a receipt giving the application number and recording the actual date (priority date) of the application. The priority date is very important in that it sets the timetable for further stages in the application process. It is the legal date for the novelty of the invention giving the application priority over all subsequently filed applications for the same invention. The same priority date may also be used for any further foreign filings as long as they are made within 12 months of the priority date.

Under the procedure at the UK Patent Office and/or the European Patent Office and/or under the Patent Co-operation Treaty, a request for a search must be lodged within 12 months from the priority date with a fee. The Patent Office searches through earlier documents looking for the same or a similar invention, as defined by the patent claims in the patent specification. The examiner provides a written search report identifying any documents which have been located that are considered material. The materials searched involve local patents and published applications, foreign patents and non-patent technical literature. No comment is made at this stage on the relevance of the documents found and neither is any indication given if other objections might be made to the application. Shortly after 18 months from the priority date, the application is published with the search report. This publication is to alert the public to the content of the application. Within six months of its publication it is necessary to lodge a request for examination of the application with a fee. There follows an examination process, which may take up to three and half years, where the Patent Office examiner uses the results of the search to determine if the invention is new, involves an inventive step and meets all of the other criteria for the grant of a patent. The responses to the examination process can be conducted by the applicant but are best performed by a Patent Attorney acting as agent for the applicant.

The grant of a patent in the UK or at the European Patent Office may take up to four to five years from the priority date. The contents of the patent application, however, are published after the first 18 months but third parties using the invention without authorisation cannot be sued for infringement until the patent is granted. Damages, however, may accrue as soon as the patent application is published and can be claimed by infringement action when the patent is granted.

Q8   Can I object   to others' patent rights?

The European Patent system includes a procedure allowing third parties to oppose the grant of a patent and interested parties may make observations in writing to the UK and European Patent Offices after the publication of the application, and before the grant of the application, concerning the patentability of an invention. The UK Patent system permits the court or the comptroller of the Patent Office to revoke a patent upon application by any person on a number of specific grounds.

Q9   Where can   patent information be found?

Patents are a very significant source of information for research and development purposes. The publication in the UK and European Patent Office of all patent applications provides a valuable source of information on the activities of competitors and potential co-operative partners identifying what new markets others are developing and which countries they see as providing their main markets.

The UK Patent Office web site (**www.patent.gov.uk**) and the European Patent Office web site (**www.european-patent-office.org**) provide access to databases of patent literature. A further method of access to online patent searches is provided by the CORDIS (European Community Research & Development Information Service) IPR help desk, which can be accessed from the CORDIS home page (**www.cordis.lu**).

Q10   What is the   difference between patent and copyright protection for computer programs?

Copyright protects the expression of the work but does not protect ideas, procedures, methods of operation or mathematical concepts as such. Computer Programs are protected as literary works under copyright whatever may be the mode or form of their expression.

Patents may be granted only for inventions that are:

■ **New.**

■ **Involve an inventive step.**

■ **Are capable of industrial application and are not a scheme, rule or method for performing a mental act, playing a game or doing business or a program for a computer as such.**

The European Patent Office Technical Board of Appeal has decided that the exclusion of computer programs as such is to be restricted to those programs which are mere abstract creations which **lack** technical character. Therefore, a computer program is patentable *if the program when running on a computer or loaded into a computer, brings about, or is capable of bringing about, a technical effect which goes beyond the 'normal' physical interactions between the program (software) and the computer (hardware) on which it is run.*

The difference between copyright and patents, therefore, as far as computer programs is concerned is that the technical effect produced by the ideas, procedures, methods of operation or mathematical concepts which are excluded from copyright protection may be granted patent protection if they are new, involve an inventive step and are capable of industrial application. This means those independently created implementations of the ideas, procedures, methods of operation and mathematical concepts embodied in an existing program that do not meet the novelty and inventive step requirements for patent protection are currently available for use by other program creators.

Q11 How is the existence of copyright proved?

Copyright will exist as soon as the program is recorded, whether in writing, on tape, on computer disk or otherwise.

Although it is not mandatory it is advisable to identify copyright ownership explicitly on disks, screen displays, print-outs and manuals. The minimum requirement for an effective copyright marking is:

© [Copyright proprietor] [year of first publication]
It is appropriate to add *All rights reserved*.

The copyright notice should also be accompanied by the following statement for licensed software on disks and screen displays.

This software may not be used, sold, licensed, transferred, copied or reproduced in whole or in part or in any manner or form except in accordance with the licence agreement provided with this software or with the prior written consent of the copyright owner.

Similar statements should be included in manuals and written material associated with a software product.

The international dimension and future developments

Q12   How similar | **are national laws about IPRs?**

Intellectual property rights are, with some rare exceptions like the Community Trade Mark, national in nature, and so they are separate national rights which must be enforced in each national court in which the right subsists and in which it has been infringed. Registered rights like patents must have been the subject of a registration process either in, or at least having effect in, every country in which it is sought to enforce them. If such a right has not been registered in a particular country there will be no associated right there to enforce. The position is different with unregistered rights. The most important such right for computer program protection, copyright, will subsist automatically in most countries of the world provided that the author is resident in or a national of a country which is a member of either the Berne Copyright Convention or of the World Trade Organisation, or, like the UK, of both.

Although most intellectual property rights are national in nature, and so have to be enforced in local courts, there is a substantial degree of harmonisation both at an international and regional level between intellectual property rights, and the harmonisation trend is set to continue. Another feature is the increasing degree to which, where there is no local precedent, courts will look to the approach of courts in other countries to the same sort of problem. This means that longer and more fully reasoned judgements from countries such as Germany, the Netherlands and the UK often assume a greater apparent importance in other countries in Europe than even local judgements.

Q13   What are the | **main trends in IP law in the UK?**

In the UK (which consists of three legal jurisdictions – England & Wales, Scotland and Northern Ireland, each of which apply the same intellectual property laws) we are at the intersection of two conflicting trends in legal harmonisation. We share a historical legal tradition with other *common law* jurisdictions such as the United States, Ireland and most of the Commonwealth; this tradition places great store on the doctrine of precedent. This is to be compared with the *civil law* tradition of Continental Europe, which is also shared by many other countries. This impacts more and more on UK law through the legal harmonisation activities of the European Commission in the field of intellectual property. The first such harmonising measure in the field of copyright in Europe was the 1991 European directive on the legal protection of computer programs (*the software directive*).

The software directive can be regarded as a success of harmonisation, because before it there was no satisfactory protection for software in some countries in Europe. However, one consequence of harmonisation arises because it is easier to harmonise intellectual property by adding new rights, or by increasing existing ones, than it is to take away or to limit rights. The result is a tendency to increase intellectual property protection even though an inadequate analysis may have been made of whether such increased protection would actually be of benefit to industry and to the public at large. One example is the increase in the term of protection resulting from the 1993 European directive on the harmonisation of copyright term. This increased the duration of copyright protection to life of the author plus 70 years from life plus 50 years. The directive took this approach because even though everywhere else in Europe had life plus 50 years, Germany had life plus 70 years and France had this for musical works. It was easier to harmonise up to life plus 70 years than to harmonise down to life plus 50 years, which would have involved complex transitional provisions to preserve existing rights in France and Germany. In response the USA has also increased its term of protection for copyright to life plus 70 years.

A current area of controversy is that over grant of patents for computer programs and for a range of other subject matters such as business methods and mathematical methods. Even though there is an exception in European patent laws which excludes *computer programs as such*, these can be patented in Europe at the European Patent Office (EPO) by presenting them as technical subject matter. National patent offices in Europe, notably that in the UK, view such patent applications less charitably. Given this disparity of approach the European Commission has indicated that it will seek to harmonise the approaches of patent offices and courts throughout Europe in this area and it is expected to introduce draft legislation early in 2000, which will probably mandate adherence to the more permissive EPO approach.

Another current example of a consequence of harmonisation in Europe is the proposal by the European Commission to mandate the introduction of a system of 'utility models' with many of the features of patents but having a shorter term (10 years rather than 20). These would lack some of the checks and balances of the patent system, like examination before grant (although rights would have to be examined before any attempt was made to enforce them). In the same way as with patents, computer programs *as such* were excluded from the initial version of the proposal, but that exclusion has been dropped in the draft submitted by the Commission in Summer 1999.

The area of software related patents is also a good example of wider international differences in approach. There are no exceptions from patentability in the USA which resemble the exceptions in Europe, with the result that software and business method patents are commonly granted in the USA. They are also now being litigated, as in the actions brought over *E-commerce patents* by amazon.com and priceline.com in the Autumn of 1999.

The individual and software IPRs

The individual as creator of software

Q14	Who owns	the rights to the program I create?

Copyright, design rights, patent rights and rights arising out of obligations of confidence can exist in relation to code, program structure, screen displays, user interfaces, design documents, manuals and information stored on the computer. As discussed in the section starting on page 6, the ownership of copyright, patent and design rights is governed by statutes and the ownership and use of all of these rights can be governed or varied by agreement.

Q15	What determines	who owns the rights to a program?

The ownership of the rights in a program (and supporting material) substantially depends on the circumstances surrounding its (their) creation. Relevant factors include:

■ **Whether the person creating the software was employed to write the program or was acting as an independent contractor;**

■ **The terms of the contract of employment or the contract between independent contractor and client.**

■ **Whether the program was written by a team or by a single person and, if by a team, whether the contribution of each person is identifiable.**

■ **What elements/sections of the program were re-used from other sources.**

As a general rule, the person who creates the program is the author of it and is the owner of the rights in it. An exception to this is where the program was produced in the course of the author's employment in which case the employer will be the owner. This can be varied by agreement between the employee and the employer. Accordingly, the immediate concern is to determine whether the work was produced in the course of the employment. To determine whether there is an employee/employer or an independent contractor/client relationship it is necessary to look at all the circumstances surrounding the relationship. Relevant factors can include the manner in which payment is made for the work that is performed and how it is taxed, the degree of control over the author, payment of insurance premiums and liability for error.

Where there is an employee/employer relationship what amounts to the *course of employment* is usually easy to determine. Problems can arise where the program has been written outside of the normal hours of employment or whether the creation of programs is outside the scope of the employee's agreed duties. For this purpose the scope of the employee's duties includes anything that the employer and employee have specifically or by implication agreed. To determine what has been agreed it is necessary to look at the duties set out in the contract of employment and at any subsequent variations to those duties (written, oral or implied).

In contrast, where there is an independent contractor/client relationship, the contractor who created the program retains ownership unless the contract between the parties provides otherwise. Identifying who owns rights in the program code and design documents can be problematic where contracts are vague, contradictory or silent as to the ownership of the program. Courts will often look at the terms of the contract and the circumstances surrounding its creation to determine whether there was an intention to transfer ownership from the contractor to the client. For instance, courts may look at whether the fee payable or the purpose for which the program was created suggests a licence or an assignment of the copyright.

Where ownership has not been dealt with by the parties courts have also implied licences into contracts to enable the party that commissioned the program to continue to use or exploit it in some defined areas (e.g. by on-sale).

Q16 What are moral rights?

These rights apply to works in which copyright subsists:

- To be identified as the author of a work.

- Not to have work subjected to derogatory treatment.

- Not to have a work falsely attributed to him/her.

The first two rights do not apply to computer programs but all three apply to works subject to copyright that can be used in the creation of programs, e.g. diagrams, instructions, design specifications/parameters. Under English law these rights cannot be assigned, but they can be waived. Accordingly, authors and employers/clients need to consider the need to give or secure waivers of these rights.

Q17 Why are confidentiality or non-disclosure agreements so important?

Confidentiality obligations, can restrict the re-use of code and design documents (i.e. the computer program and its associated documents). If the code and/or the design documents contain confidential information or if the function of the code and/or the design documents is confidential to the employer or the client then they may be able to prevent re-use. In this way an employee or contractor could be prevented from re-using the code and design documents in programs that they develop for third parties.

Obligations of confidence can arise independently of any contract, but should be dealt with in the contract that regulates the work. If code or design documents are to be re-used then it is necessary to ensure that this is not prevented by an obligation of confidence owed to the person for whom they were originally written.

Q18 **Don't situations** **get very complicated where several people create a program together?**

Often programs and design documents are produced as a result of the joint efforts of a number of people. Where each person's contribution is separate and distinct and can be identified there is usually little difficulty as each person owns the rights (subject to the points made above) in that distinct portion. However, if the contributions are not separate, distinct and identifiable the rights will be owned jointly, which will affect the way the program and design documents can be re-used.

Q19 **How can I** **ensure ownership of rights?**

To retain ownership of, or at least an interest in, the program and design documents it is sensible to deal with the issue in the contract covering the work. To avoid doubt, the contract should be in writing and signed by each party. It is wise to seek legal advice before agreeing to any contract.

Q20 **I believe** **that a former employer or client is, without my permission, re-using some code (or other design documents) in which I own the rights. What can I do?**

In the case of an employee and employer relationship the general rule is that the employer will own the rights that exist in the program and design documents written by the employee. In contrast, independent contractors often retain the rights to programs and design documents they have created. (Note that moral rights may provide limited protection in relation to design documents, refer to the comments on moral rights in Question 16 above.)

Where employees or independent contractors have retained ownership of the rights to programs and/or design documents they may be able to bring an action in court to restrain the use. This is subject to any express or implied licence that the employer or client may have to use the material. It is conceivable that an employee or independent contractor may only have the right to prevent use in narrow circumstances, for instance, where the employer's or client's licence merely extends to the use for which the program was originally drafted.

To ascertain whether the program or design documents have been used improperly the first step is to determine the extent of the employer's or client's rights and whether the conduct falls within those rights. If not, court action may be available to compel the employer or client to stop using the program and/or design documents.

Unfortunately, court actions are costly, lengthy and time consuming. Procedures for alternative dispute resolution exist, however these can also be expensive and time-consuming, although in some cases far less so than court actions. In all cases it is sensible to consider a commercial approach as strict insistence on legal rights may not be the most cost effective or time effective way to resolve the problem.

Q21 How can I be sure that I can re-use parts of a program from earlier jobs?

One way to ensure that the program and design documents can be re-used is to retain all of the rights to them. Unfortunately, this is not always a practical or an achievable goal. Where there has been an employee and employer relationship the employer will almost always own the rights in the program and design documents. Where the relationship has been between independent contractor and client there will usually have been the need to assign or, at least, license rights in the program to the client. Where it is not possible to secure ownership it is necessary to secure a licence back that enables the program and the design documents to be re-used for as many purposes as possible. The best time to deal with this issue is during negotiations over the agreement to write the program.

In the absence of an obligation of confidence, it may be possible to re-use a certain amount of the program without infringing the copyright. The reason is that copyright only prevents the copying of all or a substantial part of a program. However, this practice can cause enormous problems and result in costly disputes and, accordingly, is not recommended. It is often extremely difficult to determine what amounts to a substantial amount of any program as it is assessed qualitatively having regard to what is an important part of the program. Disputes frequently occur about the amount of copying that is permissible and practically the onus can be on the copier to establish that the amount copied is not a substantial part of the program.

Q22 What evidence can I provide that the software is my original work?

Copyright is a major form of protection for programs. The essential element of copyright is that it can be used to provide legal sanctions against copying, either conscious or, in some cases, subconscious. Copyright does not prevent independent creation. Accordingly, it is wise to keep an audit trail of all the work undertaken to show that it has not been copied from another source.

The best course of action depends on whether it is necessary to prove that someone has copied the program or to prove ownership when there is an accusation of infringement of copyright.

To answer either case, documentation of each stage of development of a program should be kept, including code which is later revised. The final code is likely to contain birthmarks such as redundant routines which were forgotten during revision, or errors which do not affect the authenticity of the program but which would need to be explained by someone claiming to own the copyright. To establish priority by date it could be useful to deposit a copy of the program with a solicitor or bank. Alternatively, good evidence can be provided by enclosing the copyright material in an envelope which is registered, sent to yourself and kept unopened.

Techniques have been developed to hide information within text, images and audio. The hidden information is sometimes called a signature or fingerprint. Various methods of installing the name of the author within data, or within a program, have been devised. Currently there is much research into methods of hiding fingerprints in images. One example is by altering the least significant bits in an array of pixels to an extent which is not visible to the human eye. These techniques come under the heading of steganography (the art of secret writing).

It may be necessary to respond to the accusation that the program has been copied and the fingerprinting added later. In this case the accuser must be challenged to show a copy that does not contain the steganographic information. For this reason the fingerprinting method must not be visible to an infringer who seeks to remove the evidence.

The individual as user of software

This covers almost everyone at work these days. It is very easy to violate someone else's rights in software, through an apparently innocent act – just copying a file from one PC to another so as to help a colleague out. The violation of a licence gives rise to civil liability. The unauthorised copying of software can be a criminal offence.

Many organisations provide guidance to staff about various aspects of computer security. This will often include prohibiting actions which would cause the organisation to pirate software. Also many organisations control their licensing of software by the use of LAN based tools which perform an audit and compare with the licences held.

Q23   **Am I free** | **to copy the software I use at work onto the laptop which I use at home and when I'm travelling?**

The software package will be protected by copyright, usually belonging to the author or authors of the package or their employer, and any unlicensed copying or use of that package will be an infringement of that copyright. Whether or not the freedom exists to copy a package used on one computer on to other computers will therefore depend on the scope of the licence for the package.

Some licences permit packages licensed by employers to be copied onto other machines used by employees under certain conditions but others do not. Thus an employee should first ask his or her employer whether or not the licence permits this. Moreover, many conditions of employment now make unauthorised copying of software that is licensed to the employer a disciplinary offence, so not consulting the employer could leave the employee open to disciplinary action.

Q24	**Can I give**	copies of programs to my friends?

As with the previous question the answer to this depends on the terms on which the program in question was licensed. If it is a commercial program with a shrinkwrap licence it is most unlikely that the licence terms will permit copies of the program to be given to third parties. However, if the program is 'shareware', as are many small programs off the web or on cover disks it is likely that its licence terms will be such as to encourage its wider dissemination in this way. But do then respect the requirements of the shareware licence as to registration and payment, and encourage people who are given copies of the program and who find it useful to do likewise.

Q25	**What do I do if**	I suspect that my employer is using unlicensed software?

This may well be inadvertent which is why it is best first to try to bring this to the employer's attention. It should be borne in mind that certain actions in relation to unlicensed use of software may involve criminal as well as civil liability.

The organisation and protection of software

The organisation as creator of software

We wish to distribute our software through a network of partners (often original equipment manufacturers or suppliers), who will share in the profit.

Q26 How can we	**ensure that our partners, often small businesses in emerging economies, respect the IPRs in our software?**

Every organisation should enter into appropriately drawn contracts with their partners. These contracts, which should be prepared by a lawyer skilled and experienced in software licensing in the partner's country, should authorise the partner to license the software only to end users, and only on terms which the organisation specifies or approves. These terms should usually include a right for the organisation to terminate any end user's licence for breach. The organisation should not allow copies of its software to be created or sold independently of the equipment on which it is to be loaded by the partner, except strictly for back-up purposes and on terms which fully protect the organisation's position.

Instead of reserving a right to terminate end user licences in the partner's country, the organisation may prefer to leave this responsibility to the partner. If the organisation does so it should ensure that it can insist on the partner discharging this responsibility, and the obligation of the partner should be clearly, firmly and enforceably stated. Bear in mind though that the organisation may cease to have a relationship with the partner, or the partner may cease to exist, long before the software has ceased to be used by end users to whom it has been provided by the partner.

Q27 We want	**to ensure world wide protection for a new software product. What is the most effective way to achieve this?**

The most readily available, and least costly, form of protection internationally is copyright. Copyright provides for national protection in all countries which are parties to the Berne Convention. National protection means that an owner of copyright in any Berne Convention country is entitled to certain minimum protection in any other Berne Convention country, in accordance with the copyright or equivalent law of that country. The Berne Convention requires that national protection be available without any registration formality in all Berne Convention countries. Most countries in the world are members of or are bound by the Berne Convention, but it is advisable to check the current national law situation.

Additionally, organisations should only distribute their products on contract terms which are appropriate and capable of being enforced in the countries in which they propose to distribute the product. Software owners may also be able to use patent, trade mark and trade secrets protection in those countries, but this will depend on the laws of each country in which they propose to distribute the product.

In distributing to overseas countries care should be taken to choose an appropriate law to govern the contracts. It is not always wise to choose the law that applies in the distributor's own country: it may be difficult to enforce those laws in other countries, and enforcing a judgement of one country's courts may equally be difficult if the defendant lives, and only has assets, in the other country.

Q28   We have been told that the database directive from the European Union sets a new standard of originality. Is this true?

A database will be protected by copyright if it is its author's own intellectual creation. The database content of databases produced by EEA database makers will be protected against unauthorised extraction or re-use of the database contents.

Q29 How can we know whether our database compilation is now protected?

A database may potentially be protected in every European Economic Area (EEA) country both by copyright and by the new sui generis right created by the Directive. The sui generis right is called database right in the UK.

Under the Database Directive:

■ **Copyright is only available to protect database compilations which are their author's *own intellectual creation*; and**

■ **The *sui generis* right is only available to protect the content of databases where the maker of the database can show that there has been qualitatively and/or quantitatively a substantial investment in either the obtaining, verification or presentation of the contents of the database.**

The Directive's new rules apply to databases according to the dates at which they were compiled or otherwise made:

■ **A database made before 27 March 1996 is entitled to copyright for the full term of copyright (usually life of author plus 70 years) under the national law then in force in the country in which the database was made, without regard to the new requirement for intellectual creativity. In the UK, the law's requirements before the Directive came into force made no reference to intellectual creativity and required only that a sufficient degree of skill, labour or experience should have been applied in the creation of the database for the database to be treated as original for copyright purposes;**

■ **A database made on or after 1 January 1983, which as at 1 January 1998 qualified for protection under the *sui generis* right, may qualify now for that right.**

■ **For all other databases the new rules have applied since 1 January 1998.**

Not all databases are classed as databases for the purposes of the new law. This provides that *database* means a collection of independent works, data or other materials which are arranged in a systematic or methodical way, and are individually accessible by electronic or other means. A collection of materials which does not fall within this definition, for example because the contents of the collection are not *independent* of one another, may still be protected under national copyright laws, and entitled to Berne Convention national protection, but not as a *database*. Such a collection cannot be protected by the new *sui generis* database right.

Q30	Where can	we go for advice?

The BCS publishes lists of qualified specialists. See Appendix D for further details. In relation to patents, patent attorneys are appropriate; in relation to trade marks, trade mark agents are appropriate; and for more general IP work and advice, solicitors (also, where appropriate, barristers) are the most likely source of skilled help and experience. Some lawyers have developed particular expertise in this area. Other consultants with experience of the IT industry may have appropriate skills and may be able to help you.

Q31	Can we	decompile (reverse engineer) program code?

Decompilation of computer programs is usually restricted by copyright law as either copying or adaptation, but is allowed in certain strictly limited circumstances:

● If carried out under a licence which allows decompilation, for example for error correction; or

● If carried out for the permitted purpose of interoperability, that is in order to obtain the information necessary to create an independent program which can be operated with the program which has been decompiled or with another program.

In this context:

● The decompilation must be carried out by a person who has a lawful right to use the program, usually a licensee;

● The information to be obtained must not be disclosed to any third party or used for any purpose other than the permitted purpose of achieving interoperability. In particular, it must not be used to create a program which is substantially similar in its expression to the program which has been decompiled, or to do any act restricted by copyright; and

● The information for which decompilation is required must not be readily available from any other source.

If carried out for the permitted purpose of achieving interoperability, under the conditions referred to above, it is immaterial that a licence or other contract forbids decompilation either generally or for that purpose. Any such contractual restriction is void.

Q32 A software tool	is vital to our business, but the author refuses to license its use to us. What can we do?

There is no general rule that a licence must be granted because it is vital to a prospective licensee's business, but a refusal to license may be a breach of European competition law, either:

● As distorting trade between Member States of the EEA; or

● As abusing a dominant position within the EEA in a particular market.

The issues are too complex to answer in a brief note, and competent legal advice is needed on your particular facts, but answers to the following may be relevant:

▌ **Does the author license the tool to your competitors or others?**

▌ **Is the tool unique in its field, so that no alternative product can be substituted?**

▌ **Is the author being a dog in a manger, that is to say withholding the tool in order to reserve a market to himself which he is never likely to satisfy?**

Q33 We suspect that	several customers are copying our software product and avoiding payment of licence fees to us. What can we do?

If you can identify those customers:

● Carefully read the licences you have granted to them, and be confident that they are not within their rights;

● Check whether your licences reserve a right for you to terminate for breach by your customers of your licence terms, or otherwise;

● If your licences reserve a right of access to your customers' premises, equipment and software, exercise this right with legal advice and obtain evidence of unlawful copying if you can do so.

Evidence may also be available from other sources:

● If you are advised by your solicitors that you are entitled to terminate those customers' licences, do so in appropriate terms. Provided the facts support you and you have taken the right steps, you may then be able to take your customers to court and to obtain an injunction (court order) prohibiting their continued use of your software. You may also be able to obtain compensation (damages) for the losses your customers have caused by their wrongful acts; but

● **Be careful:** particular facts or circumstances, of which you may not be aware, may give the customers you suspect a good answer to your allegations. If you make an unjustified claim you could yourselves be liable in legal costs, and possibly for damages as well. With assistance from FAST (The Federation against Software Theft – **www.fast.org.uk**) you may consider taking, or procuring the appropriate authorities to take, criminal proceedings against customers whom you suspect to have been unlawfully copying your software. Although this course will be cheaper than exercising your rights under the civil law, you will have less, if any, control over the process and you are unlikely to obtain compensation.

The organisation as user of software

Q34 What measures	can be taken to prevent employees from distributing software elsewhere?

Software is almost invariably provided to users on the basis of a licence from the owner of the software. This is the case whether the software is an off the shelf package like Microsoft Office™ or a bespoke application tailor made for a large organisation. The unauthorised distribution or sale of copies of the software in breach of the terms of the licence is illegal. It may give rise to claims for compensation from the owner who may also apply for a court order prohibiting further copying or sales. In some circumstances an organisation may be held responsible for the unlawful activities of its employees and may itself be liable for criminal offences as well as the individuals involved.

Preventing employees distributing software

It is therefore important for you to take steps to show that your employees are not permitted to copy or distribute software used by you and that you have done all you can to prevent them from doing so. Some examples of actions you can take:

■ Include a provision in their terms of employment prohibiting the copying of software used by you and making any such copying a serious disciplinary matter;

■ Keep original CD-ROMs and floppy disks securely and restrict access to them;

■ Restrict access to CD Writers and blank writeable CDs;

■ Openly monitor email traffic to block the distribution of electronic copies of software;

■ Limit access to installation copies of software applications held on network servers.

| Q35 | How can we | be sure that our suppliers really own IPRs in software which they provide to us? |

Because IPRs are intangible it is very difficult to be absolutely certain as to what IPRs exist, let alone who is the owner of them. If you are in a position to negotiate the terms of a software licence with a supplier then you should insist on adequate safeguards as terms of the licence:

Licence safeguards

■ A contractual promise (a warranty) by the supplier that it is the owner of the copyright and other IPRs in the software or that it is properly authorised by the owners of those rights to license them to you;

■ A warranty that the use of the software will not infringe the rights of any third party;

■ An indemnity to protect you in the event of claims by third parties that they own IPRs in the software or that its use infringes their rights.

In some cases you might wish to ask the supplier to identify the individual authors of the software and to satisfy you that they have effectively assigned their rights to the supplier or authorised it to deal in the IPRs.

| Q36 | To what extent | can I make my employees personally responsible for a properly licensed use of software? |

Your employment manual should make it clear that your employees are only permitted to use software in the course of their work which is approved by you. It should prohibit their loading any other software onto your computers. This is important not only from a licensing point of view but also to protect the organisation from virus attack.

| Q37 | What changes | is it permitted to make to licensed software in the nature of maintenance or enhancement? |

Copyright law gives the owner the right to restrict not only the copying of software but also its modification or adaptation. Maintenance and enhancement may be permitted in limited circumstances where it is necessary for the lawful use of the program and in particular where it is necessary in order to correct errors in the program.

This limited right may not be very useful unless the contract entitles you to require the owner to hand over the program's source code to enable the correction work to be done.

In any event, making changes is only permissible if the licence or other contract for the use of the program does not prohibit such activity. It is therefore possible for a copyright owner to reserve to himself the maintenance work.

Q38	**Under what**	**rules can we permit our employees to use shareware on company business?**

There is a danger that if employees are allowed to use shareware then this will encourage the use of unauthorised software generally. This in turn will give rise to risks of civil and criminal liabilities for copyright infringement. Shareware is usually made available on the basis that it is freely distributable for users to try out and evaluate but that if it is to be used in earnest then you are required to register with the author or owner and pay a registration fee. It is obviously difficult to monitor whether your employees are complying with these requirements. If a shareware utility or application is going to be used across the organisation then it may be preferable to negotiate a site licence with the owner on sensible terms.

Q39	**Does my**	**organisation come to share in the IPRs of a package which we have helped to develop by being involved in testing before general release (often called *beta testing*)?**

If you do help to develop a software package by being involved in the testing stage then in the absence of any agreement to the contrary you should be the owner of the copyright in any original program code which you write. If this program code is then incorporated into the final version of the software then you may have a joint share of the IPRs of the released version. You are unlikely to have any such interest if you merely contribute suggestions for changes or report on bugs that you discover.

A software house releasing software for beta testing is likely to do so only on the basis of written terms. These usually make it clear that the testers will not have any rights in the final program code and that any IPRs in material which the tester makes available will automatically pass to the software house.

Intellectual property rights disputes

Q40	What really	happens in IPR disputes?

Very few cases have reached the courts in the UK. In an effort to give you a glimpse of the sort of battles which are being fought behind the scenes the following brief fictional case scenarios have been created. They draw on, but are not intended to resemble, real experiences. Any resemblance to a real dispute is unintentional.

Black vs Grey

Black owned the copyright in a software package and had built up a successful business around it. Employees of Black left and set up Grey. They started to market a package which resembled that offered by Black and after a short development period the first deliveries of Grey's Package were made.

Black examined the Grey product. He decided that it bore a strong resemblance to his own product and that it was hard to believe that Grey had been able, in the short time available, to create the new product independently. There was strong suspicion that Grey had used Black's intellectual property to gain a quick start.

Computer experts were instructed to examine the Grey product. Their findings reinforced Black's suspicions – it was likely that Grey had misappropriated parts of Black's property. Faced with the expert view Grey chose to withdraw its product from the market.

Blue vs Azure

Mr O'Deneel founded Blue and developed a software controlled device for which he cultivated a good market in a large sector of industry. He then sold his company to a conglomerate and continued as Managing Director.

O'Deneel registered a new company, Azure. The launch of a competitive product was planned and its design commenced. As the date for the new product's launch became imminent large tracts of Blue's software were adopted unaltered or with minimal changes. Some modules were translated into a different computer language.

Blue obtained an Anton Piller order (now known as a *Search & Seizure Order*) as a result of which Blue's program files were found on Azure's computers.

Azure could not produce software design documents to support their claim to have developed the new product. Nor could they show evidence of legitimate possession of the standard software library to which the programs made reference. Interlocutory injunctions were obtained which effectively put Azure out of business and required O'Deneel to pay damages to Blue.

White vs Clear

White sold a package which relied heavily on statistical analysis. Skilled representatives visited customers, carrying the software in source program code form. On site, the software would be customised for the customer by the White representative.

Some of White's representatives left and formed Clear. They created a software package to compete with White's and when they started to sell it White sued, alleging breach of copyright.

Expert investigation showed that the two sets of source program code bore no resemblance to each other. That in itself would not be conclusive, but it was also clear that the entire technical architectures and designs were radically different.

White still maintained that the functionality, especially the statistical methods employed, had been copied. Expert evidence showed that in fact the statistical methods were either taken from text books or were commonplace, not original to White. An application by White for interlocutory relief was defeated and the case collapsed.

Green vs Gold

Green developed a package and retained Gold to distribute it. The package enjoyed success. In order to implement the package for individual customers, Gold was provided with the detailed file structure design. It did not otherwise have access to Green's source code.

Gold decided to create its own competitive package. There was already a market among users who were familiar with Green's package and its user interface.

Eventually Gold cancelled the deal with Green and started supplying and licensing its own package, including the results of a sales drive to existing Green customers.

When Green sued, experts were given both packages in both source code and executable form for comparison.

The two sets of source code were quite different. The two file structures were identical. Even more significantly, the user interfaces were all but identical including some very odd features in the Green system which were exactly reproduced in Gold. These features were almost certainly the result of chance in the Green system – their strange design gave no benefit. The exact replication of them in Gold's product indicated not only that the Gold programmers wished to create a system closely resembling Green's but that they had slavishly and somewhat illogically copied it.

Gold negotiated a settlement with Green.

Pink vs Scarlett

Pink developed a market leading software package after a great deal of hard work from a team with an outstanding chief programmer.

The chief programmer left Pink and set up Scarlett to supply a competitive package. The Scarlett package was demonstrated very soon after Scarlett was set up and was delivered soon after the demonstration. Pink sued Scarlett and sought an interlocutory injunction. An expert provided an affidavit in which he drew attention to the very short time available to Scarlett before the launch of their product and contrasted this to the time and effort invested by Pink. He discovered that a number of apparently erroneous results generated by the Pink program were also generated by the Scarlett program. Not unreasonably, he regarded this as evidence of copying.

In rebuttal, a Scarlett director pointed out that several of the *errors* derived in fact from errors in data supplied to both systems by a trade body whose data were relied upon throughout the industry. As to the few other genuine errors in the software, he exhibited several passages of source code which showed how they were caused. From these passages it was obvious that the causes of the erroneous results in the two programs were quite different and that the whole structures of the programs were different.

Experts instructed by Scarlett analysed the software engineering work done by Scarlett and were able to support the position taken by Scarlett's director. The *demonstration* soon after the formation of Scarlett had been merely a mock up on skeleton software. The architectures, technical designs and the codings of the two systems were radically different. The similarities in the user interface were no greater than the similarities to several other competitive systems from other sources. Scarlett had a verifiable development history of its product which established its provenance, and which also showed that the complete working product had taken much longer to produce than had appeared at first sight and was consistent with widely accepted software development metrics.

What lessons emerge from the case scenarios?

There are lessons for prospective victims of infringers in these and other cases, and for those who may be at risk of being mistakenly accused of infringing.

■ **Legal lessons**
From a legal perspective they all involve an assessment of whether a *substantial* part of the copyright work has been copied. This assessment is often the most difficult part of any copyright action where there is anything other than an exact copy. There is no objective approach to this, and rules such as *what is worth copying is worth protecting or one looks to similarities not to differences* can only take one so far. Assessment of whether or not a substantial part of the copyright work has been copied is made in respect of each of the copyright works in issue, be these specifications at differing level of detail, user screens, high level or low level program code. Thus in theory it is possible for a program specification to have been copied whilst the program code has not been copied, but then one runs into another rule – that *there is no copyright in ideas.* Drawing the line between unprotectable idea and protectable expression makes a software copyright action where there is no similarity at the level of the program code a difficult task.

Except where blatant program code copying can be found, claimants often find their pursuit of redress is much more difficult or even impossible if they themselves have not followed good software development disciplines. When a competitor creates a product by re-coding parts of the claimant's software, what the claimant has suffered is the theft of all the development work. Every software engineer knows that this accounts for a high proportion of the total work and almost the entire creative element in producing a commercial program. It is difficult for infringers to produce evidence of that effort themselves. However, the persuasiveness of this is likely to be all but eliminated if the Claimant cannot produce evidence of that investment either. Lax practice in original, honest development leaves the door wide open to infringers who deny that such effort is needed and who assert that they just sat down by their screens and composed the entire system out of their heads. The answer is to identify and safeguard all items of your intellectual property – which are probably your crown jewels.

■ Practical comments

If you decide to compete honestly with a previous employer's software product, adopt scrupulously a *clean room* regime and make sure your development work can be made visible, leaving a verifiable audit trail. That should enable you to refute any allegation of infringement.

In one case, prospective developers of new software embodying some significantly new methods were conscious of the possibility that their product might be mistakenly seen as an infringement of a former employer's product. As a precaution (and also to reassure financial backers) they invited an independent expert of standing to examine their initial designs, verify the independent sources of any common methods (such as learned papers and text books) and to produce a report on his findings. In the remote chance of the previous employer suggesting that his intellectual property had been infringed, they would supply the independent report to counter any such suspicions at minimal cost.

Another practical measure which may prove very effective is to write, very early in your development process, to the owner of rights which might be infringed. Ask if the rights owner has any objections to your plans. The result may be a useful commercial agreement, or perhaps even a letter on file that provides useful evidence that the rights owner had no objections.

Further details of actual IPR cases in English law are covered in Appendix A. Other cases can be accessed through the Reports of Patent Cases (RPC) and the Fleet Street Reports (FSR).

Dispute resolution

Q41	How can	disputes about IPRs be resolved?

In general the methods available for resolving any commercial dispute are:

- Negotiation
- Mediation
- Arbitration
- Litigation.

Q42	What is	the role of negotiation?

Negotiation between parties is a normal feature of business life and should usually be attempted in the early stages of any dispute. To negotiate effectively requires a very good understanding of the matrix of facts and of law within which the dispute has arisen.

The result of a successful negotiation will be a new agreement between the parties. With the exception of the simplest of cases professional advice should be obtained in formulating an agreement which will be legally enforceable if necessary. Such an agreement will often include a dispute resolution clause which invokes a clear process for resolving any subsequent dispute – perhaps by mediation or by arbitration.

Q43	What does	mediation mean?

Mediation has become a much used technique, over the last ten years, for resolving disputes. The usual process involves the appointment of a respected individual to be the mediator.

A date is agreed when the parties' representatives will meet with the mediator. Personal styles of mediation differ but often the mediator will use the mediation meeting for a succession of meetings, some with one party only, others with both parties present. All individuals are there with the shared goal of disposing of the dispute.

Effective mediators are good listeners and very committed to guiding their clients toward an agreement. Mediation meetings can be emotional. They can extend late into the night as a determined mediator keeps all those present focused on their shared goal. The result of a successful mediation is a new agreement between the parties. It is usual, in significant cases, for professional advisors to agree a legally effective formulation of the agreement during the week or so after a mediation meeting. Such an agreement will often include a dispute resolution clause which invokes a clear process for resolving any subsequent dispute – often by arbitration.

Q44 | What is | special about arbitration?

Arbitration shares with **litigation** the characteristic that a tribunal is presented with the facts and the law and forms a view which is then legally binding on the parties, in the form of an arbitration award or a court judgement. In either of these processes the tribunal will search for a solution which is consistent with the rights and responsibilities of the parties which arise from their contract. This is in contrast to the position in a **negotiation** or a **mediation**. In either of these whatever the parties come to agree becomes a new contract, whatever may have been their rights and responsibilities under the earlier contract.

In arbitration the tribunal will usually be a sole arbitrator or (in larger cases) a panel of three arbitrators. Arbitration has a long and respected history in areas of business as diverse as shipping, insurance and construction. It provides a flexible approach wherein the parties may wish to agree, in consultation with the tribunal, the detailed procedure to be used.

In the UK much of the arbitral experience of many decades was incorporated into the Arbitration Act of 1996. This provides an effective framework for the tribunal to respond to the needs of the parties, or when the parties are divided on an issue to form its own legally binding view. More widely, in international business, there exists a network of treaties and conventions which ensure that arbitration awards are enforceable widely throughout the world.

An arbitration reference is a private matter. This can be attractive commercially. It enables parties to resolve their dispute without bringing public attention to confidential commercial information.

Q45 | When is it | best to go to court – to litigate?

Litigation can often be the favoured way to progress an IP dispute, particularly when it is necessary to restrain a party from a course of action – perhaps the illegal copying of software.

Litigation about intellectual property disputes is likely to be expensive, complex and of long duration. It will usually involve in-house staff – managers and employed lawyers – and professional advisors – lawyers and expert witnesses. There are many potential motivations for taking legal action, including:

- Copyright infringement

- Patent infringement

- Failure to abide by the terms of a licence

- Other contractual disputes between a licensor and a licensee of IPRs.

The recent *Woolf Reforms* have led to a new set of Civil Procedure Rules. These have as their overriding objective that the court should deal with cases justly. This implies the concept of *proportionality*, which means dealing with a case in a way which is appropriate to the amount of money involved, its importance, the complexity of issues and the financial position of each party.

In the context of the new Civil Procedure Rules litigation is to be seen as a last resort. Parties are encouraged to use negotiation or mediation to reach a commercial solution.

Where a party and its advisors have a strong view that their rights have been violated, and attempts at negotiation or mediation have failed, then the court system or an arbitration reference remains the place to argue for the enforcement of those rights. Given the importance of IPRs in today's commerce the expense, management time and potential duration can be worthwhile.

Appendix A: IPR case studies

English cases on software copyright reported in the law reports date back to at least 1980, when most of such cases concerned video games. The following are a selection of recent and other significant cases of the 1990's.

Case reports can be found in either the Reports of Patent Cases (RPC, which also covers other types of intellectual property) or the Fleet Street Reports (FSR).

Unreported cases may be available on the web site of the Patents Court (part of the High Court web site).

John Richardson Computers Ltd v Flanders & another, (Ferris J, 19.2.93) ([1993] FSR 497) concerned an allegation of infringement of copyright in relation to programs for labelling and stock control for pharmacies. The program alleged to infringe ran on IBM-compatible PCs and that alleged to be infringed ran on BBC computers. Both programs had been written by the same programmer. The defendants denied copying but the Judge found there to be some limited infringement of copyright in the BBC program.

Ibcos Computers Ltd & another v Barclays Mercantile Highland Finance Ltd & another, (Jacob J, 24.2.94) ([1994] FSR 275) concerned an allegation of infringement of copyright in relation to accounting packages for agricultural dealerships. The program alleged to infringe was written by the same person who had written the program whose copyright was alleged to be infringed. The defendants denied copying and suggested that the similarities were attributable to programming style. The Judge found there to be an overwhelming inference of copying given the unexplained similarities in the source code.

Fylde Microsystems Ltd v Key Radio Systems Ltd, (Laddie J, 11.2.98) involved two preliminary issues. The first was whether the copyright in certain software was jointly owned by the plaintiff and the defendant. The second was whether, in the absence of a written contract, the defendant had an implied licence to use the software. On this second issue, the Judge held there was no such licence arising in fact or out of necessity. The plaintiff wrote software for integrated circuits in the defendant's mobile radios such as those used by security guards. The plaintiff supplied the defendant with printed circuit boards with integrated circuits pre-loaded with the software, but made no extra charge for the software. The plaintiff later found that the defendant had supplied a customer with radios installed with its software, but the boards had been sourced from a third party. There was no argument that the plaintiff had written the software. The defendant claimed joint ownership because its employee:

1. put effort into error fixing and reporting faults and bugs;

2. made a functional contribution by way of setting the specification for the software;

3. suggested what was causing some of the faults;

4. provided technical information concerning the characteristics of the hardware; and

5. set the parameters and timing within the software.

The Judge considered two matters. The first was whether the putative author had contributed the right kind of skill and labour, and secondly, whether the contribution was big enough to amount to joint ownership in the work. In this case, although the defendant's employee's contributions took a lot of time and were valuable, they did not amount to contributions to the authoring of the software.

Cantor Fitzgerald International (CFI) & another v Tradition (UK) Ltd & others (Pumfrey J, 15.4.99) is the most recent example of the courts dealing with the question of what is 'substantial' discussed in the *Flanders* and *Ibcos* cases above and in the case studies starting on page 28. The programs in issue were for bond-broking systems. The relevant programmers at Tradition had previously worked at CFI and had written CFI's program. These programmers had taken the source code of the CFI program with them when they went to work for Tradition and had it available to them when writing Tradition's program. The intention had been to design a new and improved system for Tradition, but the programmers would have used the CFI program as a fall-back had they not finished the new program in time. The defendants admitted copying 2% of CFI's program code with another 1.3% being questionable. The Judge (following *Ibcos*) set out the test in copyright:

1. in what work(s) does the plaintiff claim copyright?

2. was each such work 'original'?

3. was there copying from that work?

4. if there was, has a substantial part of that work been reproduced?

The interrelationship between originality and substantial copying was particularly important in a case such as this. A computer program is not an expression of free thought as is a human language; it must not contain error of syntax or semantic errors. The Judge recognised that this might suggest that every part of a computer program is essential to its performance and so every part, however small, is a 'substantial part' and thus be misled by following the cases on copying of literary works. More useful were the cases to do with copying of literary compilations and the taking of the plots from books. The correct approach in testing what was 'substantial' was to recognise that the function of copyright was to protect the relevant skill and labour expended by the author of the work. Thus, in relation to a computer program, the sequences of operations chosen by the programmer to achieve his object is protectable. The Judge held that one of the programmers had consulted certain modules of the CFI program and had, by the time he had finished investigating and debugging the equivalent Tradition modules, copied a substantial part of CFI's modules. He was also in breach of his obligations of confidentiality to CFI in doing so. The Judge held that another of the programmers had not copied a large and important module. CFI failed to show that the similarities of naming the variables, the sequences in which they appeared, the sequences in which those sequences appeared or the mistakes in spelling and one technical mistake, raised an inference of copying. The similarities of names and spelling could largely be ignored because the modules originated with the same programmer. He had not directly copied nor had he memorised what he had done at CFI and reproduced it for Tradition. The similarities were merely attributable to his using his skill and knowledge gained while programming for CFI. Thus, CFI failed in their allegations of infringement in respect of any of the modules which Tradition had denied copying. As Tradition had already rewritten the programs which they had admitted were copied, and had previously offered to submit to judgement in respect of such programs, their liability was limited to damages and their exposure to an adverse order as to legal costs less than it would otherwise have been.

***Mars UK Ltd v Teknowledge Ltd* (No.1) (Jacob J, 11.6.99)**
involved allegations of breach of confidence and infringement of copyright and of database right in relation to reverse engineering of EEPROMs (Electrically Erasable Programmable Read Only Memories) used in coin discriminators to enable such discriminators to be converted to work with new coins. As to the breach of confidence allegation it was held that the encrypted information in the discriminators lacked the necessary quality of confidence to found such an action, as anyone owning such a discriminator had the right to reverse engineer it in the same way as someone owning a machine had the right to dismantle it to find out how it worked. The mere fact that information had been encrypted did not render it confidential. However, as to the other allegations it was conceded that subject only to a defence of there being an implied right to repair, as to which the Judge then went on to hold that there was not in this case, the defendants had infringed both copyright and database right in coin set data and had in its reprogramming software infringed copyright in discrimination algorithms and program code.

Appendix B: Further reading

The titles included in Appendix B, together with the web addresses in Appendix C, are included to provide additional sources of useful material. These lists are by no means exhaustive but will provide valuable reference points.

Books

1 **Baker & McKenzie Guide to Intellectual Property in the IT Industry**
Baker & McKenzie and R. Hart
Sweet & Maxwell, 1998
ISBN: 0 421 61860

2 **BCS Glossary of Computer Terms, 9th edition**
Addison Wesley Longman
ISBN:0 582 36967 3

3 **Chambers & Partners' Directory – A guide to the legal profession**
Annual Guide edited by Michael Chambers
Chambers & Partners' Publishing
ISBN: 0-85514-106-9

4 **Competition Policy and Intellectual Property Rights in the Knowledge-Based Economy**
Robert D. Anderson (Ed) (1998)
University of Calgary Press
ISBN: 1895176972

5 **Computer Law**
Chris Reed (Editor), John Angel (Editor) March 2000
Blackstone Press
ISBN 1 841740160

6 **Computer Security Reference book**
K M Jackson, J Hruska, D B Parker
Butterworth-Heinemann Ltd.
ISBN: 0 7506 0357 7

7 **Computer Software: Legal Protection in the United Kingdom, 2nd edition**
H. Carr & R. Arnold
Sweet & Maxwell (1992)
ISBN: 0 421 44380 4

8 **Copinger & Skone James on Copyright**
K. Garnett, J. Rayner James & G. Davies
Sweet & Maxwell, 14th edition
ISBN: 0 421 589 108

9 **Copyright & Designs Law**
R. Merkin & J. Black
Sweet & Maxwell (loose leaf)
ISBN: 0851 21797 4

10 **Countering Counterfeiting : A Guide to Protecting & Enforcing Intellectual Property Rights**
ICC Counterfeiting Intelligence Bureau Staff (Ed) (1997)
ICC Publishing, Inc
ISBN: 9284212316

11 **Database Law, 1998**
Edited by Christopher Rees and Simon Chalton
Jordan Publishing
ISBN: 0853085102

12 **EC Competition Law and Intellectual Property Rights : The Regulation of Innovation (1998)**
Steve D. Anderman
Clarendon Press/Oxford University Press
ISBN: 0198259778

13 **Encyclopedia of Information Technology Law**
Edited by Stephen Saxby (ed)
Sweet & Maxwell
ISBN: 0 421 37 210 9

14 **From GATT to TRIPS: The Agreement on Trade-Related Aspects of Intellectual Property Rights**
Friedrich-Karl Beier and Gerhard Schricker (Eds) (1996)
John Wiley & Sons
ISBN: 3527287825

15 **Global Dimensions of Intellectual Property Rights in Science and Technology: Office of International Affairs National Research Council**
Mitchel B. Wallerstein (Ed) et al. (1993)
National Academy Press
ISBN: 0309048338

16 **Information Hiding – First Intn. Workshop, Cambridge, UK 1996**
Ross Anderson
Springer-Verlag
ISBN: 3 540 61996 8

17 | **Information Hiding – Second Intn. Workshop, Portland, Oregon, 1998**
David Aucsmith
Springer
ISBN: 0302 9743

18 | **Intellectual Property, Fourth Edition 1999**
David Bainbridge
Financial Times Pitman Publishing
ISBN: 0 273 63156 X

19 | **Intellectual Property Rights in the Global Economy**
Keith E. Maskus (1999)
Institute for Intl Economics
ISBN: 0881322822

20 | **International Copyright in Computer Program Technology**
B. Bandey
CLT Professional Publishing, (1996)
ISBN: 1 85811098 X

21 | **The Legal 500**
Annual Guide
Legalease
ISBN: 2 8708540 98

22 | **Legal Protection of Computer Programs in Europe – A Guide to the EC Directive**
B. Czarnota and R. Hart
Butterworths
ISBN: 0 406005427

23 | **Modern Law of Copyright and Designs, 2nd edition**
H. Laddie, P. Prescott and M. Vittoria
Butterworths, 2nd edition
ISBN: 040661697 3

24 | **Protecting Intellectual Property Rights: Issues and Controversies (AEI Studies, 453)**
Robert P. Benko
AEI Press
ISBN: 0844736228

25 | **The Protection of Computer Software – Its Technology and Applications, Second Edition**
Derrick Grover (1992)
Cambridge University Press
ISBN: 0 521 42462 3 – 2nd edition

26 | **World Copyright Law**
J.A.L. Sterling
Sweet & Maxwell 1998
ISBN: 0421 5829 01

Journals

1   **Computer Law and Security Report**
Elsevier
ISSN: 0267 3649

2   **Computer & Telecommunications Law Review**
Sweet & Maxwell
ISSN: 0421 6966

3   **Computers & Law**
Society for Computers and the Law
ISSN: 0140 3249

4   **Copyright World**
Lloyds of London Press
ISSN: 0950 2505

5   **Electronic Commerce and Law**
Bureau of National Affairs (BNA) (Washington)
ISSN: 1098-5190   1088-1565

6   **European Intellectual Property Review**
Sweet & Maxwell
ISSN: 0142 0461

7   **Managing Intellectual Property**
Euromoney
ISSN: 0960 5002

8   **World Intellectual Property Report**
Bureau of National Affairs (BNA) (Washington)
ISSN: 0952 7613

Law reports

1   **Fleet Street Reports (FSR)**
Sweet & Maxwell
ISSN: 0141 9455

2   **Information Technology Law Reports (ITLR)**
Lawtext Publishing
ISSN: 1365-8859

3   **Reports of Patent, Design and Trade Mark Cases (RPC)**
Sweet & Maxwell
ISSN:0800 1364

Appendix C: Web resources

1   **Centre for Computing and Social Responsibility**
Addresses the social and ethical impacts of information and communication technologies through research, consultancy and education.
http://www.ccsr.cms.dmu.ac.uk/index.html
http://www.ccsr.cms.dmu.ac.uk/resources/equality/property/

2   **The Copyright Licensing Agency**
CLA is responsible for looking after the interests of rights owners in copying from books, journals and periodicals. Information and advice.
http://www.cla.co.uk/www/about.htm

3   **The Copyright Web Site**
This site endeavours to provide real world, practical and relevant copyright information and seeks to encourage discourse and invite solutions to the myriad of copyright tangles that currently permeate the Web.
http://www.benedict.com/

4   **CORDIS**
This is the home page of the European Community Research & Development Information Service.
http://www.cordis.lu

5   **Cyberspace Law Centre**
Designed to be an evolving resource for those interested in legal issues concerning cyberspace.
http://cyber.findlaw.com/

6   **The European Patent Office**
This provides access to databases of patent literature.
http://www.european-patent-office.org

7   **Intellectual Property and the National Information Infrastructure**
A report on Intellectual Property and the National Information Infrastructure. The Report, written by the IITF Working Group on Intellectual Property Rights chaired by Assistant Secretary of Commerce and Commissioner of Patents and Trademarks Bruce A. Lehman, explains how intellectual property law applies to Cyberspace and makes legislative recommendations to Congress to fine tune the law for the digital age.
http://www.uspto.gov/web/offices/com/doc/ipnii/

8   **Intellectual Property Rights**
Action lines on innovation protection systems with the innovation programme – part of European Commission's Innovation Programme. Directorate General XIII/D/1 is mandated with the operational and

strategic aspects of intellectual property. It has been implementing various measures concerning innovation protection systems in order to create awareness and to promote the importance of intellectual property rights issues in innovation processes.
http://www.cordis.lu/ipr/home.html

9   Internet and Electronic Rights Issues
Articles and information on all the different aspects of electronic rights
http://home.earthlink.net/~ivanlove/internet.html

10   IP Worldwide
Magazine of law and policy for high technology.
http://www.ipmag.com/

11   The Patent Office
The role of the UK Patent Office is to help to stimulate innovation and the international competitiveness of industry through intellectual property rights. Has a page dedicated to the Internet
http://www.patent.gov.uk/index.html
http://www.patent.gov.uk/sinternt/index.html

12   Remedies in Domain Name Lawsuits
A lengthy article discussing intellectual property rights and the Internet – information and advice.
http://www.patents.com/pubs/jmls.sht

13   Software protection
Future and past events & publications in the field of software protection, compiled by the BCS Software Protection Specialist Group.
http://www.softprot.demon.co.uk

14   Steganography – a bibliography
This list of 405 papers on steganography was compiled by Ross Anderson and Fabien Peticolas.
http://www.cl.cam.ac.uk/fapp2/steganography/bibliography

15   The United Kingdom Law Journals Directory
The site offers a directory of addresses, including web addresses, of all major United Kingdom law journals, including on-line journals which concentrate on electronic issues.
http://www.elj.warwick.ac.uk/k

16   United States Copyright Office, The Library of Congress.
Information regarding the law of copyright in USA.
http://lcweb.loc.gov/copyright/

17   World Intellectual Property Organization
The international organisation dedicated to ensuring that the rights of creators and owners of intellectual property are protected world-wide and that inventors and authors are, thus, recognised and rewarded for their ingenuity. Site provides information and guidance.
http://www.wipo.int/

Appendix D: BCS services

1. **The BCS Consultancy Register**
   www.bcs.org.uk/consult/index.html

   As part of the responsibility conferred upon it by the Royal Charter, the British Computer Society has created a Register of members who are prepared to offer their services as consultants.

   The objectives of the Consultancy Register are:

   - to help clients of computer consultants by providing information that may be of assistance in the choice of Consultants and placing of contracts;

   - to help computer consultants by enabling them to demonstrate membership of an agreed professional register.

   For the purpose of this Register, a Consultant is defined as a person whom the Society deems competent to offer advice in the field of Information Systems or associated business issues. Those recorded in the Register are Associate Members, Members or Fellows of the Society. The Register is of relevance to work conducted anywhere in the world, unless local country law prohibits this, and is open to Society members wherever they reside.

   All BCS members registered as Consultants can be viewed at **www.bcs.org.uk/consult/index.html**

   Registration
   Registration is open to BCS professional members who satisfy the requirements set out in the Regulations governing the scheme, and costs £100.00 per annum. Full details of the Regulations are set out at the we address above.

   Consultancy Register enquiries to:
   The British Computer Society
   Consultancy Register
   1 Sanford Street
   Swindon
   Wiltshire
   SN1 1HJ

   cregister@hq.bcs.org.uk 01793 417482

2. **The BCS Register of Experts**
www.bcs.org.uk/aboutbcs/expert.htm

The Register of Experts is a specialist register maintained by the British Computer Society, which contains the names of those members who are especially qualified to act as 'expert witnesses' and who are available to provide technical assistance to solicitors and other professionals in the resolution of legal issues arising in the Information Systems field.

Admission to the Register is subject to applicants satisfying the criteria set out in relevant Regulations. The requirements for admission are, briefly, that the applicant should be a corporate member of the Society with a record of significant experience in the IS field, and should have undertaken work as an expert witness or have completed a period of pupillage with an existing practitioner. An adequate understanding of law and of court procedures is necessary and all registrants must have and maintain in force a policy of professional indemnity insurance. Registration is on an annual basis and must be renewed on 1 August each year. See website above for full details

The Register is a public document which is available to official agencies and professional firms in the legal world and to other interested bodies in order to assist in identifying those members of the Society who are able to undertake work as an expert witness in the IS field.

Further information on the Register of Experts may be obtained from BCS HQ, email: jdavies@hq.bcs.org.uk tel: 01793 417469

3. **Dispute Resolution Service**
www.bcs.org.uk/aboutbcs/dispute.htm

The information systems and services industry, having greatly expanded over the last twenty-five years, is now the source of many legal disputes. Questions of breach of contract, of fitness for purpose, of negligence and of misrepresentation are arising with increasing frequency. Intellectual property issues, such as breach of confidence and infringement of copyright in computer programs and in databases, are a fertile source of contention.

The BCS, provides a wide spectrum of dispute resolution services which are available to all parties to a dispute and their legal advisers.

Arbitration
The BCS maintains a panel of experienced arbitrators who are both corporate members of the Society (Members or Fellows) and Fellows of the Chartered Institute of Arbitrators. The President of the BCS will appoint from this panel a suitable arbitrator/arbiter on the request of the parties or where the arbitration agreement between the parties so provides.

A suitable arbitration clause which parties may wish to include in a larger agreement, such as a contract for the supply of computer services or for the licence of intellectual property, is as follows:-

> 'Any dispute or difference arising out of or in connection with this agreement shall be referred to the arbitration of a single arbitrator appointed by agreement of the parties or failing such agreement appointed by the President for the time being of the British Computer Society. The arbitration shall be governed by the provisions of the Arbitration Act 1996 or any statutory modification or re-enactment thereof'

Register of Experts

The Society maintains a register of corporate members who have met its criteria for admission to its Register of Experts. These include evidence of a significant volume of experience covering all aspects of the expert's work in litigation support and references from instructing solicitors.

Copies of the Register, which is renewed annually, are available on request.

Expert Determination

Where the parties request it, or the terms of the contract require it, the parties may select or the BCS President will nominate a member of the Register of Experts to act in the resolution of a dispute. The determination may be binding or non-binding as the parties may decide or the contract provides. When parties wish to include an appropriate clause in a contract, the recommended wording is:-

> 'Any dispute [any dispute of a technical nature] [any dispute concerning topic] shall be referred for determination by a member of the British Computer Society's Register of Experts as an adjudicator who shall act as an expert not an arbitrator; appointed by agreement of the parties or failing such agreement appointed by the President for the time being of the British Computer Society.'

Alternative Dispute Resolution (ADR)

The Society encourages parties to resolve their differences or disputes by direct negotiation, but recognises that resolution may be facilitated by the services of a qualified neutral or mediator.
The President will on the request of the parties appoint a neutral or mediator from those of the members of the Register of Experts who are also accredited as Mediators/Qualified Dispute Resolvers.

Dispute Avoidance

It is better to avoid disputes, and to prevent differences from becoming disputes, by having access to qualified advice throughout projects. The Society advocates the use of its members' services for that purpose, e.g. in the role of consulting engineers.

Terms and Conditions

The nomination services are free of charge. Members will, to the best of the President's knowledge, be independent of the parties or any relevant trade association, and be free of any conflict of interest, and will be required to decline appointment if that is not so.

The terms and conditions of engagement for any of the Society's members undertaking any of the above roles is a matter for agreement between the parties and the member. Parties should expect to pay fee rates appropriate to senior qualified professionals in a consultancy role, commensurate with the status of the member concerned within the profession.

Contact:

Mr A Lewis
Registrar
The British Computer Society
1 Sanford Street
Swindon
Wiltshire
SN1 1H

Tel: 01793 417417
Fax: 01793 480270
alewis@bcs.org.uk

Appendix E: Profiles of contributors

Simon Chalton (Consultant solicitor with Bird & Bird, Solicitors)

Simon Chalton is a Solicitor and a Consultant to Bird & Bird. His interest in computer law goes back to the late 1960s, when he contributed to the development of some of the earliest applications programs used in UK law offices.

He has held office as Chairman of the British Computer Society's Intellectual Property Committee, as Chairman of the National Computing Centre's Legal Group and as Chairman of the International Bar Association's Standing Committee on Computers and Databases. He is a Fellow of the Chartered Institute of Arbitrators, a Fellow of the American Bar Foundation and a Fellow of the Society for Advanced Legal Studies.

'Database Law', published in 1998 by Jordan Publishing, was edited by Christopher Rees and Simon Chalton and written by them and a team of authors from Bird & Bird.

Trevor Cook BSc (Partner with Bird & Bird, Solicitors)

Trevor Cook joined Bird & Bird in 1974 with a degree in chemistry from Southampton University. He was admitted as a Solicitor in 1977, joining the Intellectual Property Department of Bird & Bird, where since 1981 he has been a partner.

Trevor is Secretary to the British Copyright Council Working Group on Copyright and New Technology and is Chairman of the Intellectual Property Task Force of the Legal Affairs Committee of the British Computer Society. He is Treasurer of the British Group of the AIPPI (The International Association for the Protection of Industrial Property) and is a member of the Council of Experts of the Intellectual Property Institute and chairs its Patents Subcommittee.

Michael Gifkins BSc AKC DPhil CEng FBCS FCIArb
(Chartered Arbitrator and Consultant with Logica)

Michael Gifkins qualified originally as a physicist and then moved into industry where he has gained extensive experience of computers and telecommunications over some twenty five years. In parallel with contributing to large IT projects for a wide range of commercial and government clients, Michael has developed a special interest in the legal aspects of IT. He acts from time to time as a commercial arbitrator and has been instructed as an expert witness by leading law firms. He chairs the Law Specialist Group of the BCS and has served on the committee concerned with intellectual property for more than ten years.

Derrick Grover BSc FInstP FBCS CPhys CEng (Independent Consultant)

Before retirement Derrick Grover was a Senior Executive with the British Technology Group (BTG – formerly NRDC) where he was responsible for the transfer of electronics and information technology between universities and industry. He became interested in technological methods for protecting computer programs, founded the BCS Software Protection Specialist Group and became its chairman. Prior to the NRDC he was engaged in the research and design of electronic and digital systems in the UK and USA. He has been a member of the Intellectual Property Committee for several years, is editor of the BCS book on Software Protection and has published numerous papers in the fields of Electronics and Information Technology.

Robert Hart FBCS, CPA, EPA (Patent Attorney)

An independent intellectual property consultant. Formerly the Intellectual Property Executive for Plessey Telecommunications Ltd. The inaugural Chairman of the Copyright Committee of the British Computer Society and Chairman of the Computer Technology Committee of the Chartered Institute of Patent Agents. Used by the Commission as an Expert for the Software and Databases Directives and by the World Intellectual Property Organisation and the World Bank on projects involving the modernisation of Copyright and Patent law in Developing Nations, particularly in Eastern Europe. Visiting lecturer at Queen Mary Westfield College of the University of London. Listed WIPO Intellectual Property Dispute Resolution Mediator and Administrative Domain Name Challenge Panel member.

Ian Lowe MA Cantab (Partner with Berwin Leighton, Solicitors)

Ian Lowe is a solicitor and has been a partner with city law firm Berwin Leighton since 1986. He is a litigator and a member of the firm's Information and Communications Technology Group. He has a wide range of commercial litigation experience but deals in particular with all types of IT, technology and intellectual property disputes. He also advises on non-contentious IT, internet, ecommerce and data protection issues. He is a CEDR Registered Mediator and an associate member of the Institute of Trade Mark Attorneys.

Ron McQuaker CEng FBCS FAE ACIArb FRSA (Director of Exxel Consultants Ltd.)

After early experience in programming and systems analysis he took responsibility for delivering major pioneering systems primarily in the UK and Europe. He was seconded to the Ministry of Technology to set up the National Computing Centre where he took a leading role in its formative years. His consultancy experience covers many sectors of industry from banks to chemical plants, from large official and commercial bodies to small businesses, including both the purchasing and supply sides of the industry.
Ron McQuaker is a past President of the British Computer Society and chair of the BCS Legal Affairs Committe.

Brett Rowland BSc LLB (Lawyer with Lovells, Lawyers)

Brett Rowland is a senior lawyer in the Intellectual Property and Information Technology department at Lovells, lawyers.

He has ten years of experience in England and Australia in contentious and non-contentious information technology and intellectual property law. He has particular experience in copyright, media and patents disputes and in information technology and entertainment contracts.

He holds a Bachelor of Science from Monash University in Australia and a Bachelor of Laws from the University of Melbourne and is scheduled to complete a Master of Laws in Information Technology and Intellectual Property Law from the University of Melbourne in May 2000.

Professor Adrian Sterling LLB (Barrister and lecturer in IP law)

Adrian Sterling is an authority on international copyright, computer and data protection law. He is Professorial Fellow at Queen Mary and Westfield College, and also Visiting Professor at King's College, University of London.

He is a member of several committees of the British Computer Society (which he represents on the British Copyright Council), and is Vice-Chairman of the British Literary and Artistic Copyright Association.

His writings include, in addition to many journal articles, the full length texts The Data Protection Act 1984 (second ed., 1985), Copyright Law in the United Kingdom and the Rights of Performers, Authors and Composers in Europe (1986, Supplement 1987), Intellectual Property Rights in Sound Recordings, Film and Video (1992, Supplement 1994), and World Copyright Law (1998).

Uma Suthersanen LLB (S'pore); LLM (Lond.); PhD (Lond.)
(Lecturer in intellectual property law)

Dr. Suthersanen is a lecturer at Queen Mary Intellectual Property Research Institute, University of London. Her primary area of research is comparative copyright and design laws. Prior to her appointment as lecturer, she was the Herchel Smith Research Fellow and the FT Law & Tax Research Fellow at the Faculty of Laws, Queen Mary & Westfield College. She is also a visiting lecturer at the following institutions: SOAS, University of London; University of Maastricht; Verona Intellectual Property Centre; Université Robert Schuman, Strasbourg.